I'm Lucky to Have a Friend like You

ISBN: 978-1-68088-415-9 (previously ISBN: 978-1-59842-867-4)

Printed in China.
First printing of this edition: 2022

This book is printed on recycled paper.

This book is printed on paper that has been specially produced to be acid free (neutral pH) and contains no groundwood or unbleached pulp. It conforms with the requirements of the American National Standards Institute, Inc., so as to ensure that this book will last and be enjoyed by future generations.

Blue Mountain Arts, Inc.
P.O. Box 4549, Boulder, Colorado 80306

I'm Lucky to Have a Friend like You

Susan Polis Schutz

Blue Mountain Press™
Boulder, Colorado

I'm Lucky to Have a Friend like You

There are many people
that we meet in our lives
but only a very few
will make a lasting impression
on our minds and hearts
These people will always
listen and talk to you
They will care about your happiness
    and well-being
They will like you for who you are
and they will support you at all times
It is these rare people that we will
think of often
and who will always remain
important to us
as true friends
I am fortunate to have you
for my true friend

I Have So Many Wishes for You

I wish for you to have
people to love
people in your life
who will care about you
    as much as I do
blue skies and clear days
exciting things to do

I wish for you to have
easy solutions to any problems
knowledge to make the right decisions
strength in your values
laughter and fun
goals to pursue
happiness in all that you do

I wish for you to have
beautiful experiences
each new day
as you follow
your dreams

What Is a Friend?

A friend is
someone who is concerned
with everything you do

A friend is
someone who is concerned
with everything you think

A friend is
someone to call upon
during good times

A friend is
someone to call upon
during bad times

A friend is
someone who understands
whatever you do

A friend is
someone who tells you the truth
about yourself

A friend is
someone who knows
what you are going through at all times

A friend is
someone who refuses to listen
to gossip about you

A friend is
someone who supports you
at all times

A friend is
someone who does not
compete with you

A friend is
someone who is genuinely happy for you
when things go well

A friend is
someone who tries to cheer you up
when things don't go well

A friend is
an extension of yourself
without which
you are not complete

You Are a Dear Friend

Sometimes we are lucky enough
to meet a person
who stands out
among all the other people
as being extremely special
who knows what we
are thinking about
who is happy for us at all times
who is always there to talk to us
who cares about us selflessly
who is always truthful with us

Sometimes we are lucky enough
to meet someone who is
extremely wonderful
For me
that person
is you
my dear friend

I Love Having You to Talk To

When things are confused
I discuss them with you
until they make sense

When something good happens
you are the first person I tell
so I can share my happiness

When I don't know what to do
 in a situation
I ask your opinion
and weigh it heavily with mine

When I am lonely
I call you
because I never feel
alone with you

When I have a problem
I ask for your help
because your wiseness helps
me to solve it

When I want to have fun
I want to be with you
because we have such a
great time together

When I want to talk to
someone
I always talk to you
because you understand me

When I want the truth about
something
I call you
because you are so honest

It is so essential
to have you in my life

You Are One of the Best Friends I've Ever Known

Best friends always
remember so well
all the things they did together
all the subjects they discussed
all the mistakes they made
all the fun they had

Best friends always remember
how their friendship
was such a stabilizing force
during confusing times
in their lives

Best friends may have
    different lifestyles
live in different places
and interact with different people
but no matter how much
their lives may change
their friendship remains the same

I know that throughout my life
wherever I am
I will always
remember so well
and cherish our friendship
as one of the best
I have ever known

Whatever I say
means more when
you listen
Whatever I think
means more when
you understand
Whatever I do
means more when
you are there
Whatever happens to me
means more if
I can share it with you
Thank you for
adding so much
to my life

Knowing that you are always here
to understand and accept me helps me
get along in the confused world. If every
person could have someone just like you,
the world would become a peaceful garden.

You Are the Definition of a Real Friend

Some people will be your friend
because of whom you know
Some people will be your friend
because of your position
Some people will be your friend
because of the way you look
Some people will be your friend
because of your possessions

But the only real friends
are the people who will be
    your friends
because they like you for how
    you are inside
That is the true meaning of
    friendship
I want to thank you for being
one of the very few people in
    my life
who is a real friend

If You Ever Need to Know That Someone Cares...

Sometimes we do not feel
like we want to feel
Sometimes we do not achieve
what we want to achieve
Sometimes things happen
that do not make sense
Sometimes life leads us in directions
that are beyond our control
It is at these times most of all
that we need someone
who will quietly understand us
and be there to support us

If ever things are not
going well for you
and you have some problems to solve
If ever you are feeling confused
and don't know the right thing to do
If ever you are feeling frightened
and hurt
or if you just need someone
to talk to
please remember that
I am here for you at all times
without judgment
and with understanding
and love

People are only complete
when they have a true friend
to understand them
to share all their
passions and sorrows with and
to stand by them
throughout their lives

When two people share a real friendship, they learn not only to appreciate another human being, but they also learn to understand themselves better.

You Are a Person of Strength and Courage Whom I Admire So Much

Strong people have confidence in themselves
They have a very strong sense of purpose
They never have excuses for not doing something
They always try their hardest for perfection
They never consider the idea of failing
They work extremely hard toward their goals
They know who they are

Strong people understand their weaknesses
as well as their strong points
They can accept and benefit from criticism
They know when to defend what they are doing
They are creative
They are not afraid to be a little different
in finding innovative solutions
that will enable them to achieve their dreams

Thank You for Being So Nice

You are a rare person
You are always so considerate of people —
putting their needs in front of yours
You are always so kind —
treating people in such a caring way
If everyone were like you
the world would be so peaceful

Though people are often too busy
to stop and thank you
I hope you can feel the respect and love
that everyone has for you
And though many times
I have wanted to thank you
I never got around to it
So right now
I want to emphasize my thanks to you
for being such a
nice person

You Are a Remarkable Woman and Friend

You are a remarkable woman
who accomplishes so much as a
strong woman
in a man's world
You are strong but soft
strong but caring
strong but compassionate

You are a remarkable woman
who accomplishes so much
as a giving woman
in a selfish world
You give to your friends
to your family
to everyone

You are a remarkable woman
and you are loved by
so many people
whose lives you have touched
including mine

My Best Friend

I have other friends
whom I talk to
but it's not
the same
You have such
a deep understanding
of who I am
I hardly have to
speak any words
and you know just
what I am saying

I want to be sure
you know that
no matter where I go
whom I meet
or what I do
I'll never find
as deep a friendship
with anyone as I
have with you

You have known me
in good and
bad times
You have seen me
when I was happy
and when I was sad
You have listened to me
when what I said was intelligent
and when I talked nonsense
You have been with me
when we had fun
and when we were miserable
You have watched me
laugh
and cry

You have understood me
when I knew what I was doing
and when I made mistakes
Thank you for
believing in me
for supporting me
and for always being ready
to share thoughts together

Our Friendship Will Never Change

Some friendships
change with time
Some friendships
dissolve with time
It doesn't matter
what we do or
what we are or
where we live or
how we think
Our friendship
grows deeper and stronger
with time

We have formed
a friendship
that has become
invaluable to me
We discuss our goals
and plan our future
We express our fears
and talk about our dreams
We can be very serious
or we can just have fun
We understand each other's lives
and try to encourage each other
in all that we do
We have formed
a friendship
that makes our lives
so much
nicer

You Will Always Be My Friend

You will always be my friend
when I am happy
or when I am sad
when I am all alone
or when I am with people
You will always be my friend
if I see you today
or if I see you a year from now
if I talk to you today
or if I talk to you a year from now

You will always be my friend
      and though through the years
we will change
it doesn't matter what I do
or it doesn't matter what you do
Throughout our lifetime
you will always be my friend

We Have a Lifetime Friendship

Though we may not see each other
very much
or write to each other very much
or phone each other very much
I always know that, at any time
I could call, write or see you
and everything would be exactly
the same
You would understand everything
I am saying
and everything that I am thinking

Our friendship does not depend
on being together
It is deeper than that
Our closeness is something inside of us
that is always there
ready to be shared with each other
whenever the need arises

It is such a comfortable and warm feeling
to know that
we have such a lifetime
friendship

About the Author

Susan Polis Schutz is an accomplished writer, poet, documentary filmmaker, and advocate for women's issues, the elderly, and dispelling the stigma of mental illness. She is a graduate of Rider University where she majored in English and biology and was later awarded an honorary doctor of laws degree. Together with her husband, Stephen Schutz, she cofounded Blue Mountain Arts, a popular publisher known for its distinctive greeting cards, gifts, and poetry books.

Susan is the author of many best-selling books of poetry illustrated by Stephen, including *To My Daughter with Love on the Important Things in Life*, which has sold over 1.8 million copies. Its companion volume, *To My Son with Love*, has also enjoyed a wide audience. Susan's poems and Stephen's artwork have been published on over 435 million greeting cards worldwide.

Susan's latest undertaking is creating documentary films that make a difference in people's lives with her production company, IronZeal Films. Her films have been shown on PBS stations throughout the country and include *The Misunderstood Epidemic: Depression*, which seeks to bring greater attention to this debilitating illness, and *Over 90 and Loving It*, which features people in their 90s and 100s who are living extraordinary and passionate lives. Her newest film, *Love wins over hate*, explores the lives of six former white supremacists and ultraconservatives. Each tells of their transformation from being filled with hate, anger, and rage to acceptance and appreciation of diversity.